How I Save The Earth

By Hilary Ego

SAVE ENERGY

I turn off the lights when leaving the room.

Energy is often created from air polluting sources, such as burning coal or gas. When I save energy, I reduce the usage of air polluting energy and help keep the air clean.

REUSE

I reuse a durable metal bottle instead of a single use disposable plastic bottle.

Reusing prevents waste from ending up in the landfill and energy waste from recycling. While recycling a one-time use disposable plastic bottle is good, it still uses air polluting energy to melt down and create a new bottle.

SAVE WATER

I turn off the water when brushing my teeth.

The Earth has a small supply of fresh drinking water. When you save water, you conserve our limited natural water resources and help prevent future droughts.

RECYCLE

I recycle clean and empty glass jars, metal cans, plastic containers, cardboard boxes, and papers.

The Earth has a limited amount of natural resources. When I recycle, I save glass, metal, plastic, cardboard, and paper from going into the landfill.

RIDE A BICYCLE

I ride a bicycle instead of using a gasoline powered car.

A bicycle provides clean transportation compared to gasoline powered cars. By riding a bicycle instead of a car, I exercise and prevent air pollution.

PLANT TREES

I plant trees in my yard, neighborhood, and community.

Trees provide many environmental benefits, including: creating oxygen, cleaning the air of harmful air pollutants, providing shade to save energy, and beautifying neighborhoods.

GREAT WORK

I'm ready to teach my family and friends about how they can save the Earth too!

About the Author

As an environmental sustainability professional, Hilary is passionate about teaching and empowering people to help save the Earth. With her education and industry experience, Hilary shares easy environmental tips and explains the positive impact of each action. She hopes this book will inspire readers to share with friends and family how they help save the Earth!